The Night of the Elephants

Level 5 – Green

Helpful Hints for Reading at Home

The graphemes (written letters) and phonemes (units of sound) used throughout this series are aligned with Letters and Sounds. This offers a consistent approach to learning whether reading at home or in the classroom.

HERE IS A LIST OF NEW GRAPHEMES FOR THIS PHASE OF LEARNING. AN EXAMPLE OF THE PRONUNCIATION CAN BE FOUND IN BRACKETS.

Phase 5			
ay (day)	ou (out)	ie (tie)	ea (eat)
oy (boy)	ir (girl)	ue (blue)	aw (saw)
wh (when)	ph (photo)	ew (new)	oe (toe)
au (Paul)	a_e (make)	e_e (these)	i_e (like)
o_e (home)	u_e (rule)		

HERE ARE SOME WORDS WHICH YOUR CHILD MAY FIND TRICKY.

Phase 5 Tricky Words			
oh	their	people	Mr
Mrs	looked	called	asked
could			

GPC focus: /wh/ph/

TOP TIPS FOR HELPING YOUR CHILD TO READ:

- Allow children time to break down unfamiliar words into units of sound and then encourage children to string these sounds together to create the word.

- Encourage your child to point out any focus phonics when they are used.

- Read through the book more than once to grow confidence.

- Ask simple questions about the text to assess understanding.

- Encourage children to use illustrations as prompts.

This book focuses on the phonemes /wh/ and /ph/ and is a green level 5 book band.

The Night of the Elephants

Written by
Emilie Dufresne

Illustrated by
Silvia Nencini

"Neema, you are on me!" says Bem as he pulls his leg from under her. Neema pushes into the corner.

"I cannot help it – I am an elephant!" Neema says with a grin. Bem feels a push of Neema's trunk.

Neema rests on the mud and is soon asleep. Her trunk whispers and snorts. Bem curls up next to her.

"Neema, that is it! You are too big for the den!" says Zev. Neema gets up and whips round.

Bem says, "Neema might be an elephant, but she is part of the pack too, no matter what she is!"

"Bem, I do not fit in the den so I cannot be a part of this pack. I must go," says Neema.

Neema steps round the pack with a humph. She steps on the meerkats as she storms from the den.

Neema stands in the light of the moon. She whacks the shrubs with her foot as she stomps.

Neema is in a sulk when she sees a light far off. It is a dolphin. It seems to be a phantom.

The phantom looks at Neema. With short steps, Neema turns to the gold, glittering thing. It looks across the grass at her.

Bem creeps into the grass. At the end of the grass, Neema sees the dolphin whizz off.

The dolphin jumps up and down in a pool of gold. It stops under a tree. The dolphin says something.

"Neema, you are an orphan, yes?" says the dolphin.
"How did you –" says Neema.
"You seek the elephants," says the dolphin.

"We will go to the Night of the Elephants. You must keep along this trail," says the dolphin.

At that, the dolphin starts to morph into a ring of light. Then it shoots off into the night.

Bem looks at Neema as she starts to go along the gold trail left by the glittering dolphin. He starts to go, too.

As she stomps across the plains,
Neema meets the alpha. Bem holds back.
Neema has not seen Bem yet.

The alpha stomps up to the dust and paws at it. "Neema, what is this?" he asks.

"I am going to the Night of the Elephants to meet my pack," says Neema.
"Good luck," says the alpha.

She plods and plods. The end of the light is at the top of a cliff. A twig cracks. She turns.

"Neema, you are part of the pack!" says Bem.
"But what if the elephants are my pack?" says Neema.

"I will not stop you. We will still be your pack, no matter what you do," says Bem.

In the light of the moon, they rest on the mud and look into the night. "Look! Elephants!" says Bem.

They sit. There is no sound. They look at the elephants. Then Neema says, "Shall we go back to the den?"

"But the elephants?" says Bem.
"My pack are not the elephants.
My pack are all tails and hair…"

They go back to the den. Zev says, "Look! We dug all night, so now we will all fit in the den."

The Night of the Elephants

1. What noises did Neema's trunk make when she was sleeping?

2. What does Neema whack with her foot as she stomps?
   a. Shrubs
   b. Stones
   c. Grass

3. What is an 'orphan'?

4. Why do you think Neema didn't join the other elephants?

5. How do you think Neema felt when she saw that her pack had dug a bigger den for her? Have you ever felt like Neema did?

©2021 **BookLife Publishing Ltd.**
King's Lynn, Norfolk PE30 4LS

ISBN 978-1-83927-405-3

All rights reserved. Printed in Malaysia.
A catalogue record for this book is available from the British Library.

The Night of the Elephants
Written by Emilie Dufresne
Illustrated by Silvia Nencini

An Introduction to BookLife Readers...

Our Readers have been specifically created in line with the London Institute of Education's approach to book banding and are phonetically decodable and ordered to support each phase of Letters and Sounds.

Each book has been created to provide the best possible reading and learning experience. Our aim is to share our love of books with children, providing both emerging readers and prolific page-turners with beautiful books that are guaranteed to provoke interest and learning, regardless of ability.

BOOK BAND GRADED using the Institute of Education's approach to levelling.

PHONETICALLY DECODABLE supporting each phase of Letters and Sounds.

EXERCISES AND QUESTIONS to offer reinforcement and to ascertain comprehension.

BEAUTIFULLY ILLUSTRATED to inspire and provoke engagement, providing a variety of styles for the reader to enjoy whilst reading through the series.

AUTHOR INSIGHT:
EMILIE DUFRESNE

Born in Québec, Canada, Emilie Dufresne's academic achievements explain the knowledge and creativity that can be found in her books. At a young age, she received the award of Norfolk County Scholar, recognising her top grades in school. At the University of Kent, Emilie obtained a First Class Honours degree in English and American Literature, and was awarded a Masters in The Contemporary with Distinction. She has published over 60 books with BookLife Publishing, in subjects ranging from science to geography, art and sports, and even animals as superheroes! Children enjoy Emilie's books because of the detailed narrative and the engaging way she writes, which always entices children to want to learn more.

This book focuses on the phonemes /wh/ and /ph/ and is a green level 5 book band.